THE HORRORS
OF DATING

ILLUSTRATED BY
NASTKA DRABOT

A COLORING BOOK

HARPER
Celebrate

TO: _____

FROM: _____

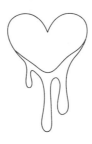

TO THOSE WHO HAVE BEEN BURNED,
HAUNTED, AND GHOSTED LOOKING FOR LOVE,
MAY YOU FIND CATHARSIS IN THESE PAGES.

THE STAGE-FIVE CLINGER

ADDS YOU ON EVERY SOCIAL MEDIA SHE CAN FIND.

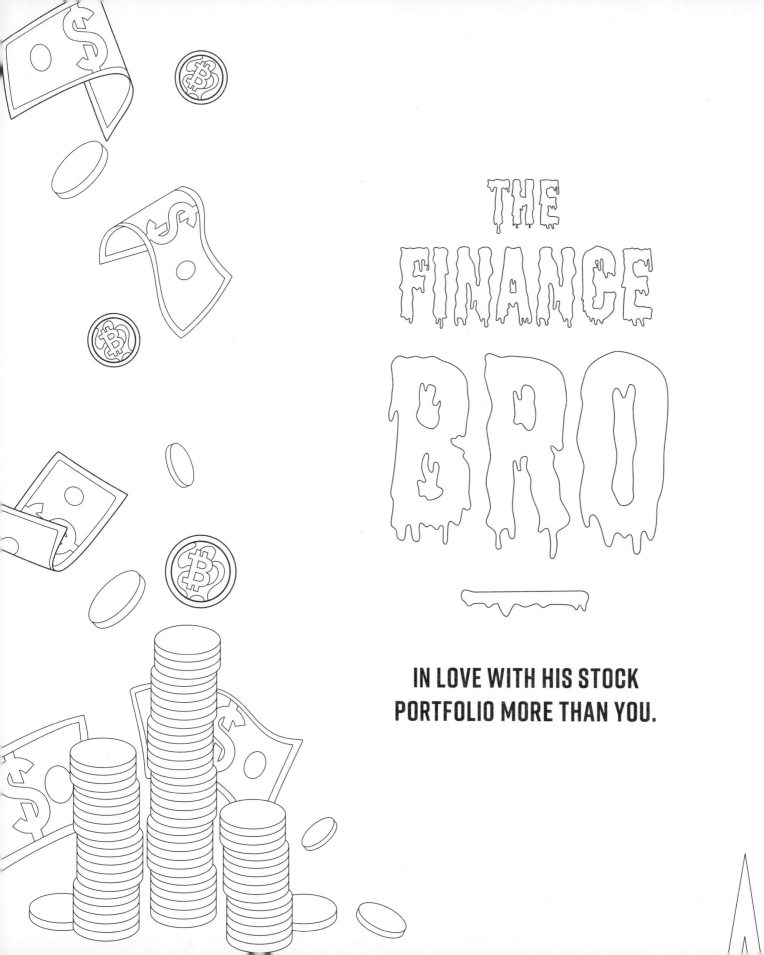

THE FINANCE BRO

IN LOVE WITH HIS STOCK
PORTFOLIO MORE THAN YOU.

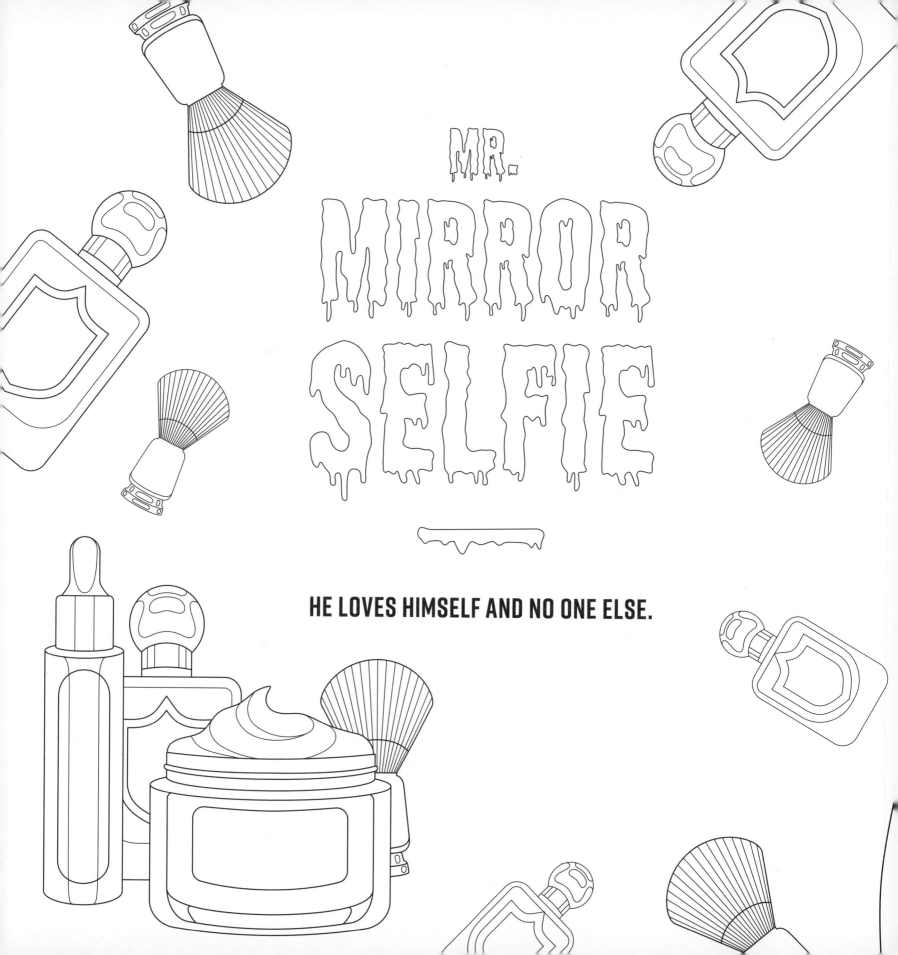

MR. MIRROR SELFIE

HE LOVES HIMSELF AND NO ONE ELSE.

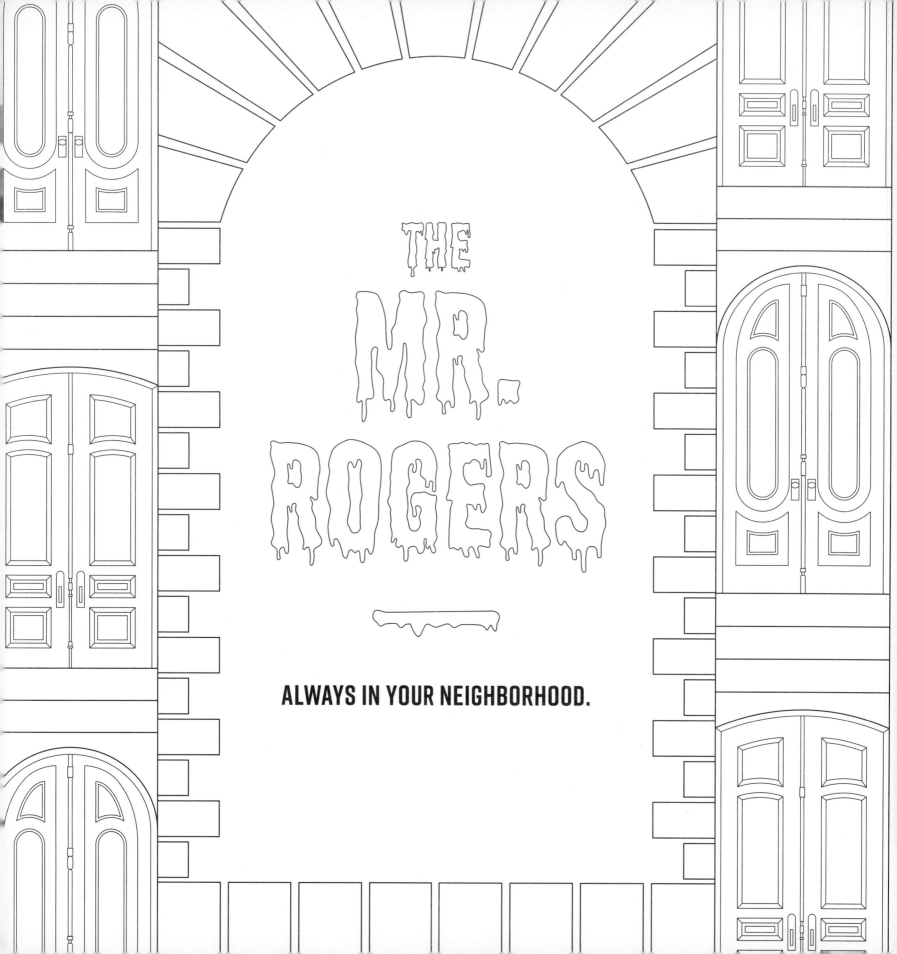

THE MR. ROGERS

ALWAYS IN YOUR NEIGHBORHOOD.

THE GUESS WHO?

GROUP PHOTOS GALORE . . .
BUT WHICH ONE IS SHE?

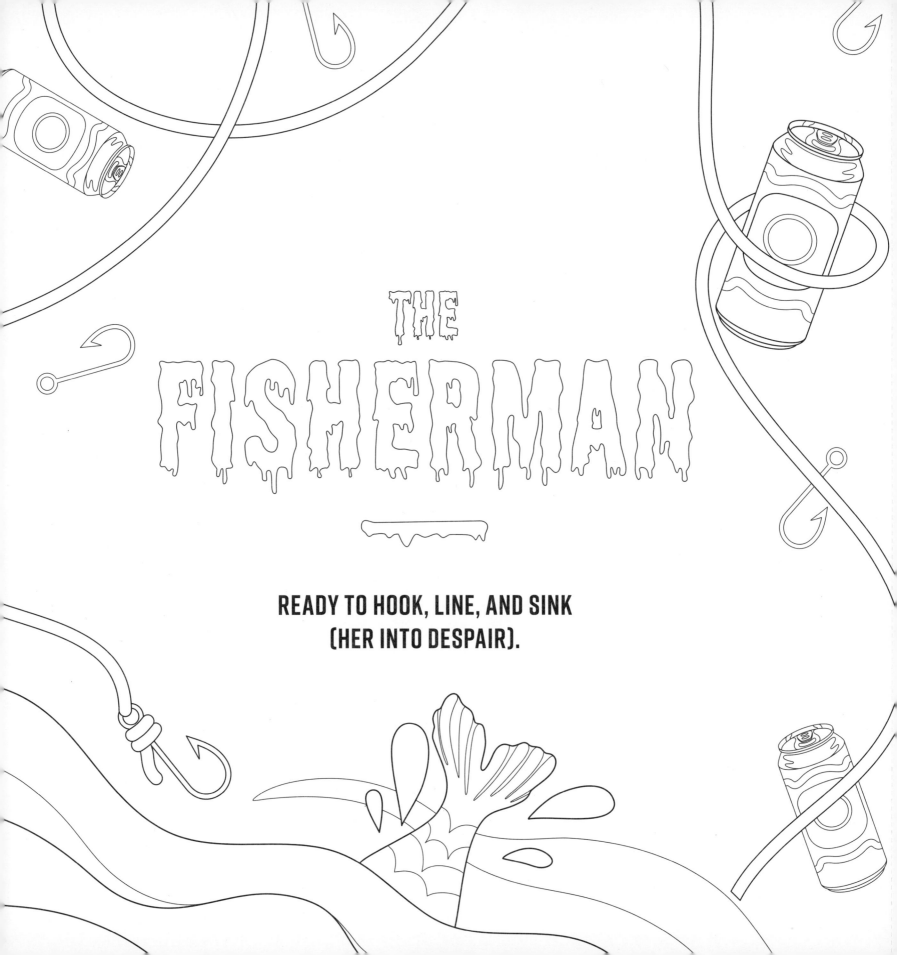

THE FISHERMAN

**READY TO HOOK, LINE, AND SINK
(HER INTO DESPAIR).**

HAT GIRL

**WHY DO THEY ALL
WEAR THE SAME DANG HAT?**

THE ASTROLOGIST

**READS YOUR BIRTH CHART BEFORE
SHE EVEN CONSIDERS COCKTAILS.**

THE GHOSTER

AT LEAST YOU HAVE SOME TIME TO YOURSELF?

THE INFLUENCER

ONLY DATING YOU FOR THE VIEWS AND THE LIKES.

THE BACHELORETTE WANNABE

SHE'S IN IT FOR THE WRONG REASONS.

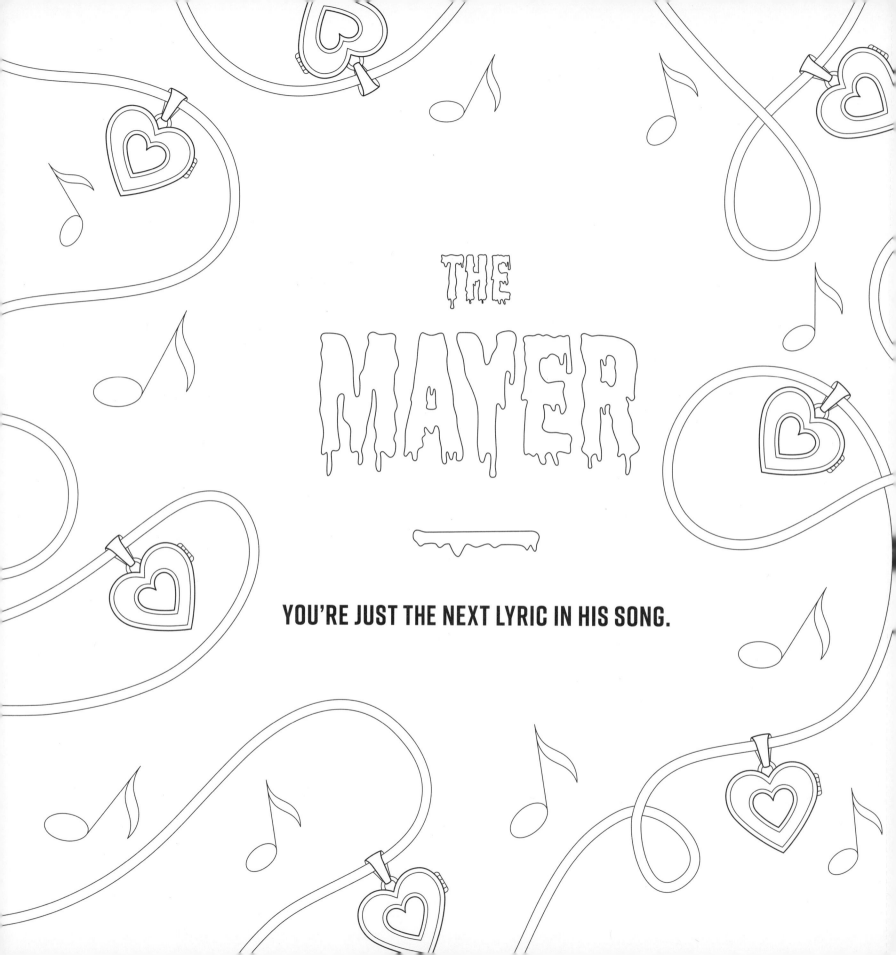

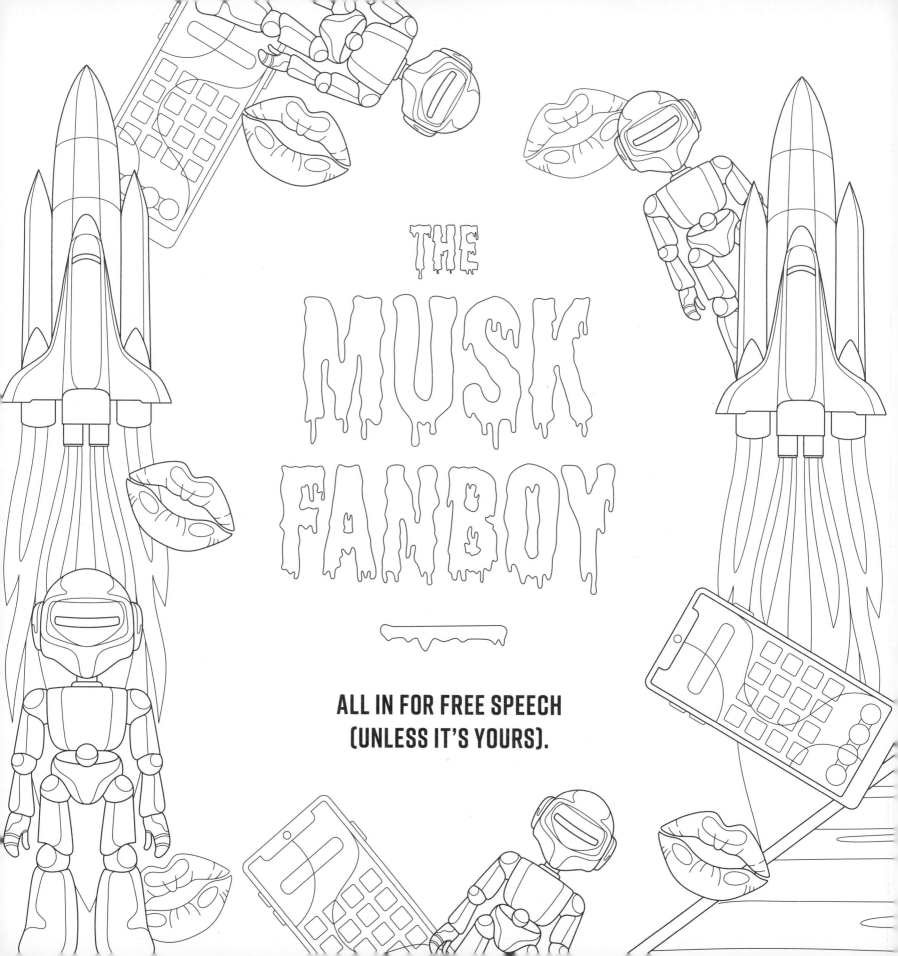

MRS.
FILL IN THE
BLANK
—⌣—

**READY TO COMMIT TO
ANY LAST NAME SHE CAN.**

THE COACH

ALWAYS LOOKING TO ADD TO HIS ROSTER.

THE ROYAL

**LOOKING FOR A LOYAL SUBJECT
TO WAIT ON HIM HAND AND FOOT.**

THE SELF-EMPLOYED CEO

SO, I'M HEARING NO BENEFITS.

HELP YOURSELF

YOU'RE SO HOT:
100 REASONS WHY
HUSTLE

FINDING VALIDATION IN MY WORK
BECAUSE I CAN'T FIND IT IN MY
RELATIONSHIPS

WINNING

THE JET-SETTER

**TELL ME MORE ABOUT THAT SEMESTER
ABROAD TEN YEARS AGO!**

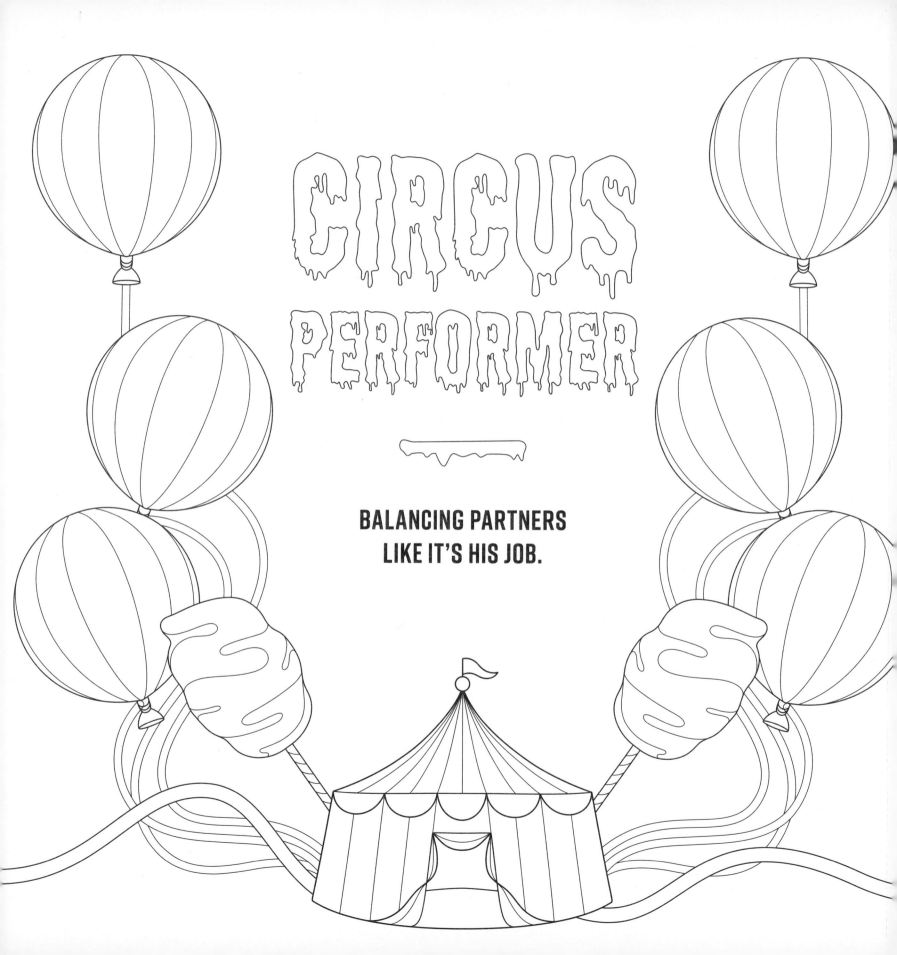

CIRCUS
PERFORMER

BALANCING PARTNERS
LIKE IT'S HIS JOB.

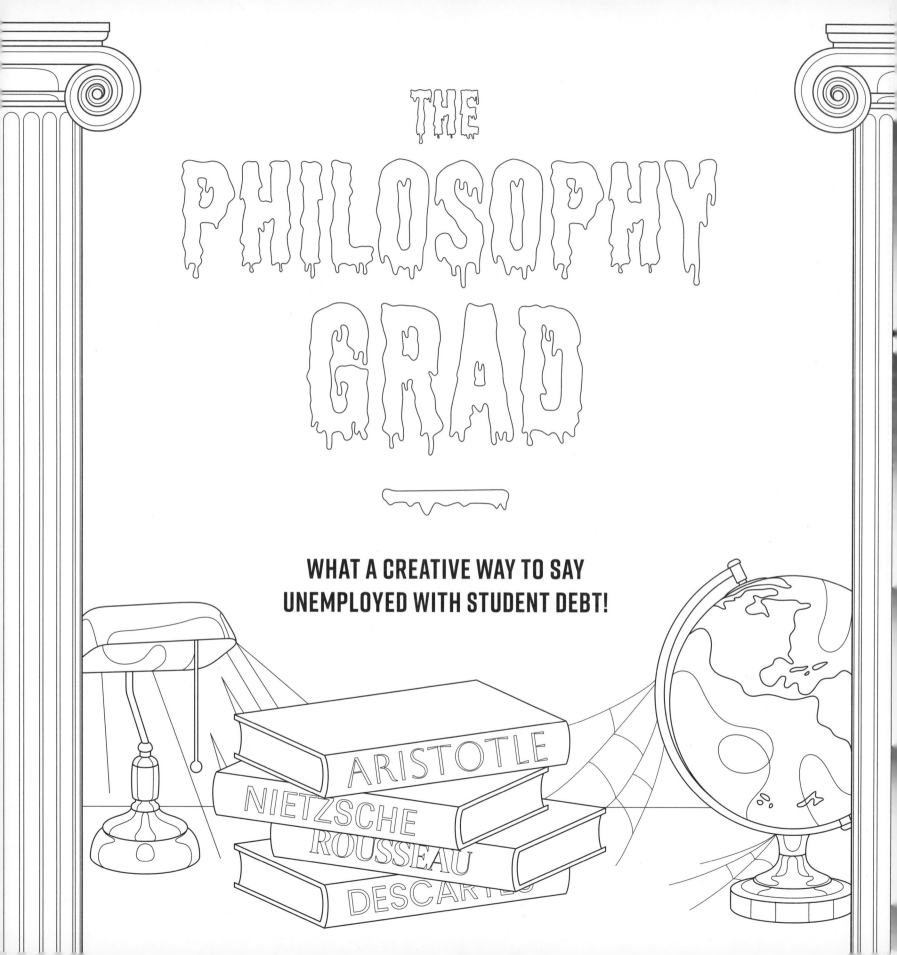

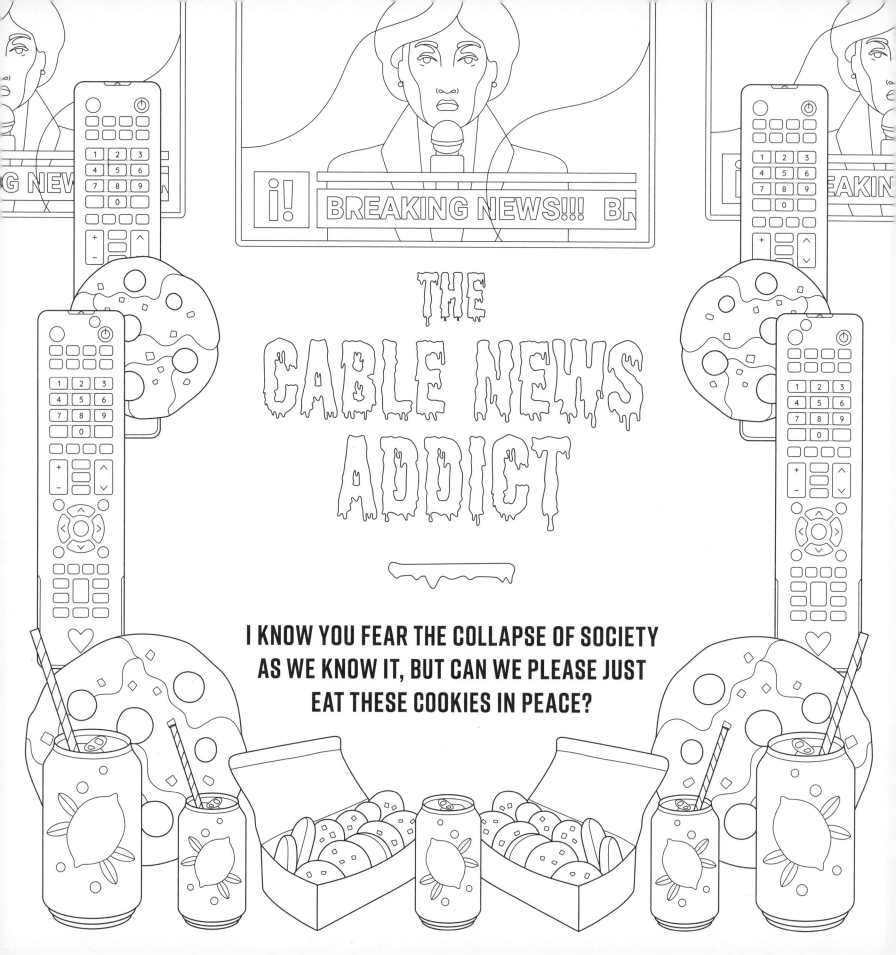

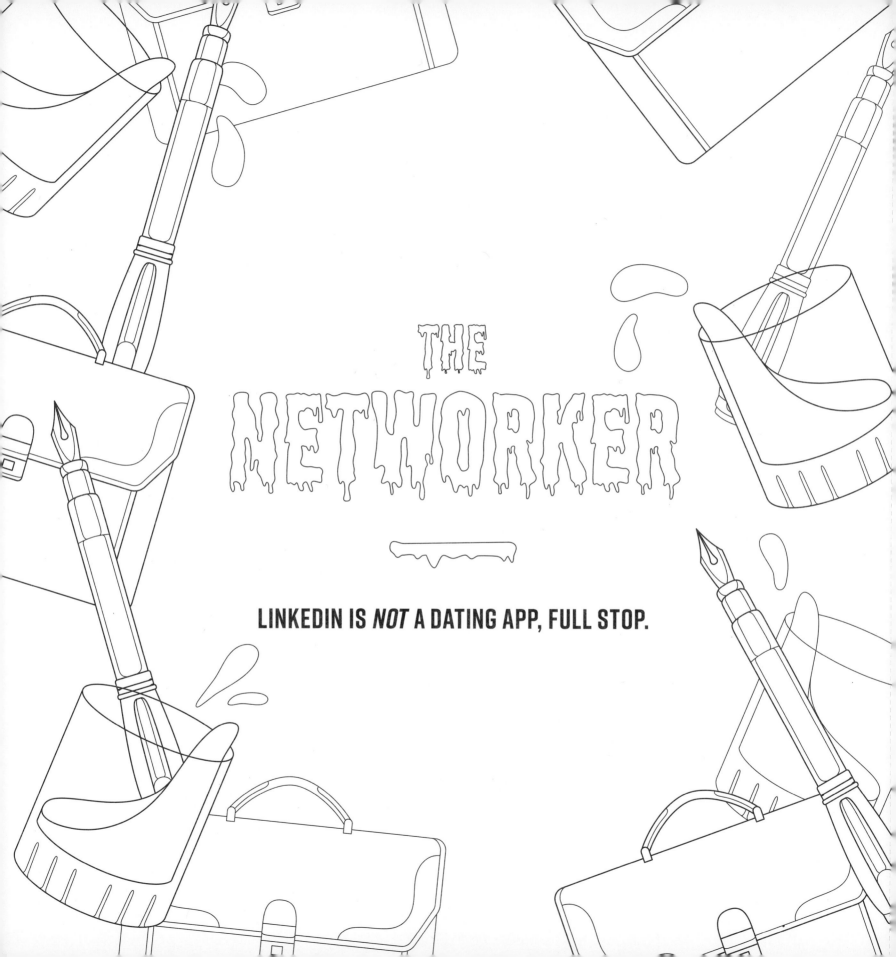

THE NETWORKER

LINKEDIN IS *NOT* A DATING APP, FULL STOP.

MR. TOO MUCH, TOO SOON

NO TALKING ABOUT CHILDREN ON THE FIRST DATE, THANKS.

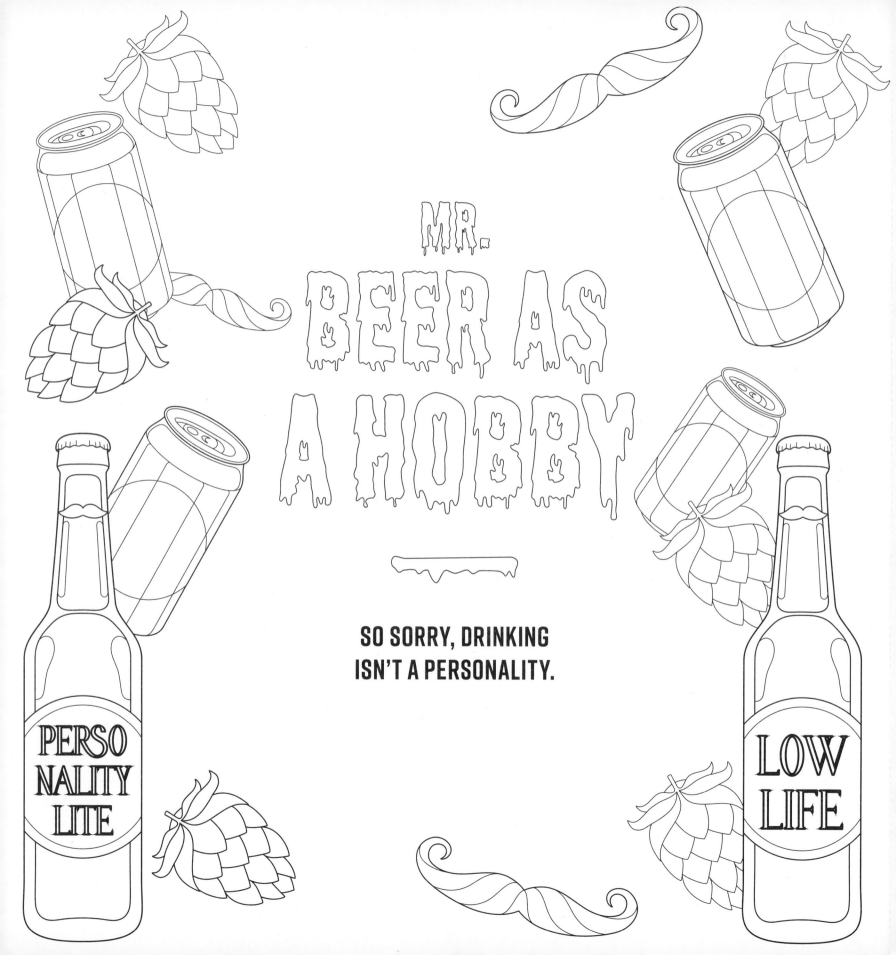

MR. BEER AS A HOBBY

—

**SO SORRY, DRINKING
ISN'T A PERSONALITY.**

PERSO NALITY LITE

LOW LIFE

THE TIME TRAVELER

I SEE YOUR FRESHMAN YEAR PHOTOS, BUT WHAT DO YOU LOOK LIKE NOW?

GOLDILOCKS

NOTHING IS EVER *JUST RIGHT*.

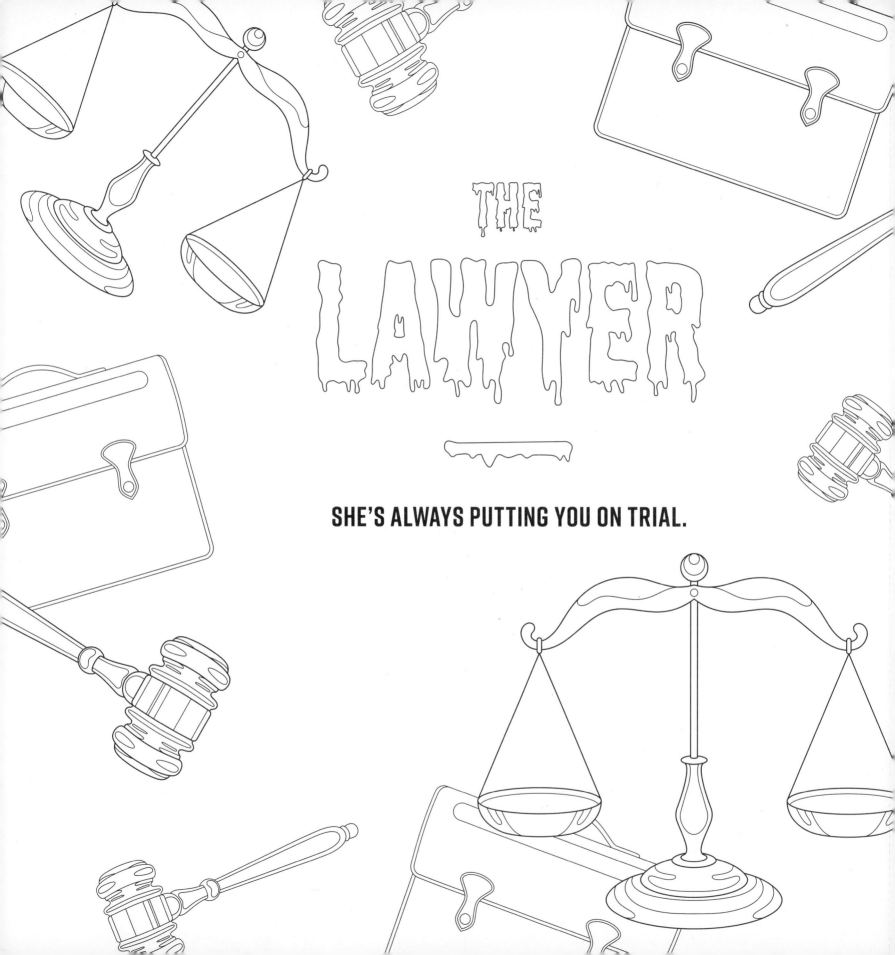

THE LAWYER

SHE'S ALWAYS PUTTING YOU ON TRIAL.

THE KNIGHT IN SHINING ARMOR

**NO ONE WAS IN DISTRESS
UNTIL HE SHOWED UP.**

THE ENERGY VAMPIRE

SUCKING YOUR WILL TO LIVE ONE DATE AT A TIME.

THE BOOMERANG

OH MY GOSH, WHY DO YOU
KEEP COMING BACK?

THE SUN

MY LIFE DOESN'T, IN FACT,
REVOLVE AROUND YOU, BABE.

FORTUNE TELLER

HAS A VISION FOR YOUR FUTURE TOGETHER
BEFORE YOU EVEN TELL HER YOUR LAST NAME.

THE FIGMENT OF YOUR IMAGINATION

BUT YOU KNOW WHAT, THEY'RE GREAT!

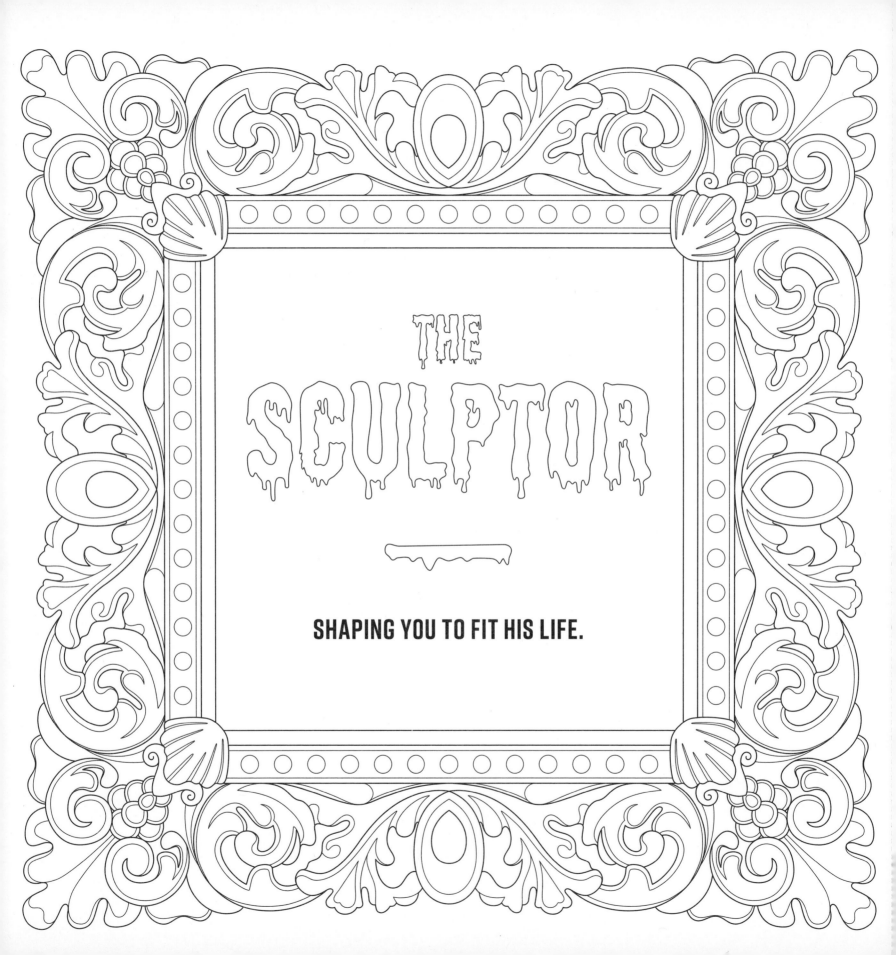

THE SCULPTOR

SHAPING YOU TO FIT HIS LIFE.

THE JANE AUSTEN

**LOOKING FOR HER DARCY,
BUT THE THING IS,
SHE'S NO ELIZABETH.**

THE QUARTERBACK

I MEAN, COOL?

THE FREUDIAN SLIP

NO, I DON'T COOK LIKE YOUR MOM, AND NO, I WON'T APOLOGIZE.